BELIEVE IN
YOURSELF

Maple Spring Publishing Titles

BELIEVE IN YOURSELF

FEATURES
BONUS
BOOK: RICHES ARE YOUR RIGHT

JOSEPH MURPHY

MAPLE SPRING PUBLISHING

Published 2024 by Maple Spring Publishing

Front cover design by David Rheinhardt of Pyrographx

Interior design by Meghan Day Healey of Story Horse, LLC.

Library of Congress Cataloging-in-Publication Data is available upon request

ISBN: 979-8-3505-0066-0

10 9 8 7 6 5 4 3 2 1

Contents

1

Make Your Dreams Come True

J oseph, in the Bible, means "disciplined or controlled imagination." It is one of the primal faculties of mind, and has the
power to project and clothe your ideas, giving them visibility on
the screen of space.

Israel loved Joseph. *Israel* is the spiritually awakened man who
knows the power of controlled imagination. It is called the "son
of his old age." Son means "expression." *Old age* implies wisdom
and knowledge of the laws of mind. When you become familiar
with the power of imagination, you will call it "the son of your old
age." Age is not the flight of years; it is really the dawn of wisdom
and Divine knowledge in you. *Imagination* is the mighty instrument used by great scientists, artists, physicists, inventors, archi-
tects, and mystics. When the world said, "It is impossible; it can't
be done," the man with imagination said, "It *is* done!" Through
your imagination, you can also penetrate the depths of reality and
reveal the secrets of nature.

A great industrialist told me one time how he started in a small
store. He said that he used to dream (Joseph was a dreamer) of a
large corporation with branches all over the country. He added

that regularly and systematically he pictured in his mind the giant building, offices, factories, and stores, knowing that through the alchemy of the mind, he could weave the fabric out of which his dreams would be clothed.

He prospered, and began to attract to himself—by the universal law of attraction—the ideas, personnel, friends, money, and everything needed for the unfoldment of his ideal. He truly exercised and cultivated his imagination, and lived with these mental patterns in his mind until imagination clothed them in form.

I particularly liked one comment that he made as follows: "It is just as easy to imagine yourself successful as it is to imagine failure, and far more interesting."

Joseph is a dreamer, and a dreamer of dreams. This means he has visions, images, and ideals in his mind, and knows that there is a Creative Power that responds to his mental pictures. The mental images we hold are developed in feeling. It is wisely said that all our senses are modifications of the one-sense-feeling. Thomas Troward, a teacher of mental science, said, "Feeling is the law, and the law is the feeling." Feeling is the fountainhead of power. We must charge our mental pictures with feeling in order to get results.

We are told, "Joseph dreamed a dream, and told it to his brethren, and they hated him." Perhaps as you read this, you have a dream, an ideal, a plan, or purpose that you would like to accomplish. *To hate* is to reject in Bible language. The thoughts, feelings, beliefs, and opinions in your mind are the brethren that challenge you, belittle your dreams, and say to you, "You can't; it is impossible. Forget it!"

Perhaps other thoughts come into your mind that scoff at your plan or ambition. You discover that there is a quarrel in your mind with your own brethren; opposition sets in. The way to handle the opposition in your mind is to detach your attention from sense evidence and the appearance of things, and begin to think clearly and with interest about your goal or objective. When your mind is engaged on your goal or objective, you are using the creative law of mind, and it will come to pass.

"Lo, my sheaf arose, and also stood upright; and, behold, your sheaves stood round about, and made obeisance to my sheaf." Lift your ideal or desire up in consciousness. Exalt it. Commit yourself wholeheartedly to it. Praise it; give your attention, love, and devotion to your ideal; and as you continue to do so, all the fearful thoughts will make obeisance to your exalted state of mind—that is, they will lose their power and disappear from the mind.

Through your faculty to imagine the end result, you have control over any circumstance or condition. If you wish to bring about the realization of any wish, desire, or idea, form a mental picture of fulfillment in your mind; constantly imagine the reality of your desire. In this way, you will actually compel it into being. What you imagine as true already exists in the next dimension of mind, and if you remain faithful to your ideal, it will one day objectify itself. The master architect within you will project on the screen of visibility what you impress on your mind.

Joseph (imagination) wears a coat of many colors. A *coat* in the Bible is a psychological covering. Your psychological garments are the mental attitudes, moods, and feelings you entertain. *The coat of many colors* represents the many facets of the diamond, or your capacity to clothe any idea in form. You can imagine your friend who is poor living in the lap of luxury. You can see his face light up with joy, see his expression change, and a broad smile cross his lips. You can hear him tell you what you want to hear. You can see him exactly as you wish to see him—that is, he is radiant, happy, prosperous, and successful. Your imagination is the coat of many colors; it can clothe and objectify any idea or desire. You can imagine abundance where lack is, peace where discord is, and health where sickness is.

"His brethren said to him, 'Shalt thou indeed reign over us?'" Imagination is the first faculty, and takes precedence over all the other powers or elements of consciousness. You have 12 faculties or brethren, but your imagination, when disciplined, enables you to collapse time and space and rise above all limitations. When you keep your imagination busy with noble, Godlike concepts and ideas, you will find that it is the most effective of all faculties in your ongoing spiritual quest.

The phrase "Joseph is sold into Egypt" means that your concept or desire must be subjectified (Egypt) first before it becomes objectified. Every concept must go "down into Egypt," meaning into the subjective where the birth of ideas takes place.

"Out of Egypt have I called my son": Joseph is the commander of Egypt, which tells you that imagination controls the whole conceptive realm. Whatever prison you may be in, whether it is the prison of fear, sickness, lack, or limitation of any kind, remember that Joseph is the commander in prison and can deliver you. You can imagine your freedom, and continue to do so until it is subjectified; then, after gestation in the darkness, the manifestation comes—your prayer is answered.

Consider for a moment a distinguished, talented architect; he can build a beautiful, modern, 20th-century city in his mind, complete with super highways, swimming pools, aquariums, parks, and so on. He can construct in his mind the most beautiful palace the eye has ever seen. He can see the building in its entirety completely erected before he ever gives his plan to the builders. Where was the building? It was in his imagination.

With *your* imagination, you can actually hear the invisible voice of your mother even though she lives 10,000 miles from here. You can also see her clearly, and as vividly as if she were present; this is the wonderful power you possess. You can develop and cultivate this power and become successful and prosperous.

Haven't you heard the sales manager say, "I have to let John go, because his attitude is wrong"?

The business world knows the importance of "right attitude."

I remember many years ago having printed a small article on reincarnation. These pamphlets were on display on a book counter of a church where I lectured. In the beginning, very few of them were sold because the salesgirl was violently opposed to its contents.

I explained the biblical meaning of reincarnation to her, the origin of the story, and what it was all about. She understood the contents of the drama, and became enthusiastic about the booklets; they were all sold before my lecture series was completed. This was an instance of the importance of the right mental attitude.

Your *mental attitude* means your mental reaction to people, circumstances, conditions, and objects in space. What is your relationship with your co-workers? Are you friendly with people, with animals, and with the universe in general? Do you think that the universe is hostile, and that the world owes you a living? In short, what is your attitude?

The emotional reaction of the above-mentioned girl was one of deep-seated prejudice. That was the *wrong attitude* in selling books; she was biased against the book and the writer.

You can develop the right mental attitude when you realize that nothing external can upset you or hurt you without your mental consent. You are the only thinker in your world; consequently, nothing can move you to anger, grief, or sorrow without your mental consent. The suggestions that come to you from the outside have no power whatsoever, except that you permit them to move you in thought negatively. Realize that you are master of your thought-world. Emotions follow thought; hence, you are supreme in your own orbit. Do you permit others to influence you? Do you allow the headlines in the newspapers, the gossip, or the criticism of others to upset you or bring about mental depression? If you do, you must admit that you are the cause of your own mood; you created your emotional reaction. Your attitude is wrong.

Do you imagine evil of others? If you do, notice the emotion generated in your deeper self; it is negative and destructive to your health and prosperity. Circumstances can affect you only as you permit them. You can voluntarily and definitely change your attitude toward life and all things. You can become master of your fate and captain of your soul (subconscious mind). Through disciplined, directed, and controlled imagination, you can dominate and master your emotions and mental attitude in general.

If you imagine, for example, that another person is mean, dishonest, and jealous, notice the emotion you evoke within yourself. Now reverse the situation. Begin to imagine the same person as honest, sincere, loving, and kind; notice the reaction it calls forth in you. Are you not, therefore, master of your attitudes?

In reality, the truth of the whole matter is that it is your real concept of God that determines your whole attitude toward life in general. Your dominant idea about God is your idea of life, for God is life. If you have the dominant idea or attitude that God is the Spiritual Power within you responsive to your thought, and that, therefore, since your habitual thinking is constructive and harmonious, this Power is guiding and prospering you in all ways, this dominant attitude will color everything. You will be looking at the world through the positive, affirmative attitude of mind. Your outlook will be positive, and you will have a joyous expectancy of the best.

Many people have a gloomy, despondent outlook on life. They are sour, cynical, and cantankerous; this is due to the dominant mental attitude that directs their reaction to everything.

A young boy of 16 years going to high school said to me, "I am getting very poor grades. My memory is failing. I do not know what's the matter." The only thing wrong was his attitude. He adopted a new mental attitude by realizing how important his studies were in gaining entrance to college in order to become a lawyer. He began to pray scientifically, which is one of the quickest ways to change the mentality.

In scientific prayer, we deal with a principle that responds to thought. This young man realized that there was a Spiritual Power within him, and that It was the only Cause and Power. Furthermore, he began to claim that his memory was perfect, and that Infinite Intelligence constantly revealed to him everything he needed to know at all times, everywhere. He began to radiate love and goodwill to the teachers and fellow students. This young man is now enjoying a greater freedom than he has known for several years. He constantly imagines the teachers and his mother congratulating him on all "A's." It is imagining the desired results that has caused this change of attitude toward his studies.

We have said previously that all our mental attitudes are conditioned by imagination. If you imagine that it is going to be a black day today, that business is going to be very poor, that it is raining, that no customers will come into your store, that they have no money, and so on, you will experience the result of your negative imagery.

One time a man was walking the streets of London, and he imagined that he saw a snake on the street. Fear caused him to become semi-paralyzed. What he saw *looked* like a snake, but he had the same mental and emotional reaction as if it were a snake.

Imagine whatsoever things are lovely, noble, and of good report, and your entire emotional attitude toward life will change. What do you imagine about life? Is it going to be a happy life for you? Or is it one long series of frustrations? "Choose ye whom ye will serve."

You mold, fashion, and shape your outer world of experience according to the mental images you habitually dwell on. Imagine conditions and circumstances in life that dignify, elevate, please, and satisfy. If you imagine that life is cold, cruel, hard, bitter; and that struggle and pain are inevitable, you are making life miserable for yourself.

Imagine yourself on the golf course. You are free, relaxed, and full of enthusiasm and energy. Your joy is in overcoming all the difficulties presented by the golf course. The thrill is in surmounting all the obstacles.

Now let us take this scene: Imagine yourself going into a funeral parlor. Notice the different emotional responses brought forward as you picture yourself in each of the above-mentioned situations. In the funeral chapel, you can rejoice in the person's new birthday. You can imagine the loved one surrounded by his or her friends in the midst of indescribable beauty and love. You can imagine God's river of peace flooding the minds and hearts of all present. You can actually ascend the heavens of your own mind wherever you are; this is the power of your imagination.

"And he dreamed yet another dream, and told it his brethren, and said, 'Behold, I have dreamed a dream more; and behold, the sun and the moon and the eleven stars made obeisance to me.'"

In ancient symbology, the sun and the moon represent the conscious and subconscious mind. The 11 stars represent the 11 powers in addition to imagination. Here again, the inspired writers are telling you that disciplined imagination takes precedence over all other faculties of the mind, and controls the direction of the conscious and subconscious mind. Imagination is first and foremost; it can be scientifically directed.

I was examining one of the Round Towers of Ireland with my father over 50 years ago. He said nothing for one hour, but remained passive and receptive, seeming to be in a pensive mood. I asked him what he was meditating on. This is the essence of his answer: He pointed out that it is only by dwelling on the great, wonderful ideas of the world that we grow and expand. He contemplated the age of the stones in the tower, then his imagination took him back to the quarries where stones were first formed. His imagination unclothed the stones. He saw with the interior eye the structure, the geological formation, and the composition of the stone, and reduced it to the formless state; finally, he imagined the oneness of the stones with all stones and with all life. He realized in his Divine imagery that it was possible to reconstruct the history of the Irish race from looking at the Round Tower!

Through the imaginative faculty, this teacher was able to see the invisible men living in the Tower and to hear their voices. The whole place became alive to him in his imagination. Through this power, he was able to go back in time when there was no Round Tower there. In his mind, he began to weave a drama of the place from which stones originated, who brought them, the purpose of the structure, and the history connected with it. As he said to me, "I am able to almost feel the touch and hear the sound of steps that vanished thousands of years ago."

The subjective mind permeates all things; it is in all things, and is the substance from which they are made. The treasure house of eternity is in the very stones comprising a building. There is nothing inanimate; all is life in its varied manifestations. (The sun and the moon make obeisance to Joseph—imagination.) Truly through your faculty of imagination, you can imagine that the invisible secrets of nature are revealed to you; you will find that you can plumb the very depths of consciousness.

The other night I sat in a park and looked at the setting sun. Suddenly I began to think that the sun is like a house in the city of Los Angeles; there is a greater sun behind our sun, and so on to infinity. It staggers the imagination to ponder and meditate on the myriads of suns and solar galaxies extending into infinity beyond the milky way. This world is only a grain of sand in the infinite seashore. Instead of seeing the parts, let us look at the wholeness, the unity of all things. We are, as the poet said, "all parts of one stupendous whole, whose body nature is, and God the soul."

It is really out of the imaginative mind of man that all religions are born. Is it not out of the realm of imagination that television, radio, radar, super jets, and all other modern inventions came?

Your imagination is the treasure house of infinity, which releases to you all the precious jewels of music, art, poetry, and inventions. You can look at some ancient ruin, an old temple, or pyramid, and reconstruct the records of the dead past. In the ruins of an old church yard, you can also see a modern city resurrected in all its beauty and glory. You may be in a prison of want or lack, or behind stone bars, but in your imagination you can find an undreamed-of measure of freedom.

Remember how Chico, the Parisian sewer cleaner, imagined and lived in a paradisaical state of mind called the seventh heaven even though he never saw the light of day?

Bunyan, in prison, wrote the great masterpiece *Pilgrim's Progress*. Milton, although blind, saw with the interior eye. His imagination made his brain a ball of fire, and he wrote *Paradise Lost*. In this way he brought some of God's paradise to all people everywhere.

Imagination was Milton's spiritual eye, which enabled him to go about God's business whereby he annihilated time, space, and matter, and brought forth the truths of the Invisible Presence and Power.

A genius is a man who is in rapport with his subconscious mind. He is able to tap this universal reservoir and receive answers to his problems; thus, he does not have to work by the sweat of his brow. In the genius type of mind, the imaginative faculty is developed to a very high degree. All great poets and writers are gifted with a highly developed and cultivated imaginative faculty.

I can now see Shakespeare listening to the old stories, fables, and myths of his day. I can also imagine him sitting down listing all these characters in the play in his mind . . . then clothing them one by one with hair, skin, muscle, and bone; animating them; and making them so much alive that we think we are reading about ourselves.

Use your imagination and go about your Father's business. *Your Father's business* is to let your wisdom, skill, knowledge, and ability come forth; and bless others as well as yourself. You are about your Father's business if you are operating a small store, and in your imagination you feel you are operating a larger store giving a greater measure of service to your fellow creatures.

If you are a writer of short stories, you can be about your Father's business. Create a story in your mind that teaches something about the golden rule, then pass that story and all its characters through your spiritualized and highly artistic mentality; your article will be fascinating and intensely interesting to your public.

The truth about man is always wonderful and beautiful. When writing a novel or story we should be sure that we clothe Truth in her garment of loveliness and beauty. You could now look at an acorn, and with your imaginative eye construct a magnificent forest full of rivers, rivulets, and streams. You could people the forest with all kinds of life; furthermore, you could hang a bow on every cloud. You could look at a desert and cause it to rejoice and blossom as a rose. "Instead of the thorn shall come up the fir tree, and instead of the briar shall come up the myrtle tree." Men gifted with intuition and imagination find water in the desert, and they create cities where formerly other men only saw a desert and a wilderness.

An architect of a city sees the buildings and fountains already in operation before he ever digs a well or builds a house. "I will make the wilderness a pool of water, and the dry land springs of water."

Long hours, hard labor, or burning the midnight oil will not produce a Milton, a Shakespeare, or a Beethoven. People accomplish great things through quiet moments, imagining that the invisible things from the foundation of time are clearly visible.

You can imagine the indescribable beauty of He Who Is being expressed on your canvas, and if you are a real artist in love with beauty, great beauty will come forth effortlessly. Moments of great inspiration will come to you; it will have nothing to do with perspiration or hard mental labor.

In Greenwich Village, I met a poet who wrote beautiful poems; he had them printed on cards, and sold them at Christmastime. Some of these poems were beautiful gems of spiritual love. He said that when he got still, the words would come into his mind accompanied by a lovely scene. Flowers, people, and friends would come clearly into his mind. These images spoke to him. They told him their story. Oftentimes the entire poem, song, or lullaby would appear complete and ready in his mind without the slightest effort. His habit was to imagine that he was writing beautiful poems that would stir the hearts of men.

Shelley said that poetry was an expression of the imagination. When the poet meditates on love and wishes to write on love, the Invisible Intelligence and Wisdom within him stirs his mind; casts the spell of God's beauty over him; and awakens him to God's Eternal Love so that his words become clothed with wisdom, truth, and beauty.

The Great Musician is within. If it is your business to play music or compose music, be sure that you are about your Father's Business. Your Father's Business is first of all to recognize God as the Great Musician; then meditate, feel, pray, and know that the Inner Music sings or plays through you the Song of God's Love, and you will play like you have never played before.

Every invention of Edison's was first conceived in his imagination. The same was true of Tesla, another great inventor and scientist.

I think it was Oliver Wendell Holmes who said that we need three-story men who can idealize, imagine, and predict. I believe it was the capacity to imagine and dream that caused Ford to look forward to putting the world on wheels.

Your capacity to imagine causes you, and enables you, to remove all barriers of time and space. You can reconstruct the past or contemplate the future thought through your inner eye. No wonder it says in Genesis: "Israel loved Joseph [imagination] more than all his brethren." Imagination, when disciplined, spiritualized, controlled, and directed, becomes the most exalted and noblest attribute of man.

I was in a conversation some years ago with a young chemist who stated that his superiors for years had tried to manufacture a certain German dye and failed. He was given the assignment when he went with them. As he commented, he did not know that it could not be done, and synthesized the compound without any difficulty. They were amazed and wanted to know his secret. His answer was that he imagined he had the answer. Pressed further by his superiors, he said that he could clearly see the letters "Answer!" in blazing red color in his mind; then he created a vacuum underneath the letters, knowing that as he imagined the chemical formula underneath the letters, the subconscious would fill it in. The third night he had a dream in which the complete formula and the technique of making the compound was clearly presented.

"Joseph [imagination] is a dreamer, and a dreamer of dreams." "They conspired against him to slay him. And they said one to another, 'Behold, this dreamer cometh.'" Perhaps as you read these Biblical quotations there are thoughts of fear, doubt, and anxiety conspiring in your own mind to slay or kill that desire, ideal, or dream of yours. You look at conditions or circumstances, and fear arises in your mind; yet there is the desire within you which, if realized, would bring you peace and solve your problem.

You must be like Joseph and become a practical dreamer. Decide to make your dreams come true. Withdraw, and take away your attention now from appearances of things and from sense evidence. Even though your senses deny what you pray for, affirm that it is true in your heart. Bring your mind back from its wandering after the false Gods of fear and doubt, to rest in the Omnipotence of the Spiritual Power within you. in the silence and quietude of your own mind, dwell on the fact that there is only One Power and One Presence. This Power and Presence is now responding to your thought as guidance, strength, peace, and nourishment for the soul. Give all your mental attention to recognizing the absolute sovereignty of the Spiritual Power, knowing that the God-Power has the answer and is now showing you the way. Trust It, believe in It, and walk the earth in the Light. Your prayer is already answered.

All of us read the story of Columbus and his discovery of America. It was imagination that led him to his discovery. His imagination plus faith in a Divine Power led him on and brought him to victory.

The sailors said to Columbus, "What shall we do when all hope is gone?" His reply was, "You shall say at break of day, 'Sail on, sail on, and on.'" Here is the key to prayer: Be faithful to the end; full of faith every step of the way, and persisting to the end, knowing in your heart that the end is secure because you saw the end.

Copernicus through his vivid imagination revealed how the earth revolved on its axis, causing the old astronomical theories to be discarded.

I think it would be a wonderful idea if all of us from time to time recast our ideas, checked up on our beliefs and opinions, and asked ourselves honestly, "Why do I believe that? Where did that opinion come from?" Perhaps many ideas, theories, beliefs, and opinions that we hold are completely erroneous, and were accepted by us as true without any investigation whatever as to their truth or accuracy. Because our father and grandfather believed in a certain way is no reason why we should.

One woman said to me that a certain idea she had must be true because her grandmother believed it. That is absurd! The race mind believes in many things that aren't true. What came down from generation to generation is not necessarily valid, or the final word and authority.

The above-mentioned woman, who was honest, and well-meaning, had a mind that was very touchy on psychological truths. She took everything in the Bible literally. This mind worked by prejudice and superstition, and opposed everything that was not in accord with her established beliefs, opinions, and preconceived notions.

Our mind must be like a parachute. The latter opens up; if it does not, it isn't any good. Likewise, we must open our eyes and minds to new truths. We must hunger and thirst after new truth and new knowledge, enabling us to soar aloft above our problems on the wings of faith and understanding.

The famous biologists, physicists, astronomers, and mathematicians of our day are men gifted with a vivid, scientific imagination. For instance, Einstein's theory of relativity existed first in his imagination.

Archeologists and paleontologists studying the tombs of ancient Egypt through their imaginative perception reconstruct ancient scenes. The dead past becomes alive and audible once more. Looking at the ancient ruins and the hieroglyphics thereon, the scientist tells us of an age when there was no language. Communication was done by grunts, groans, and signs. The scientist's imagination enables him to clothe this ancient temple with roofs; and surround them with gardens, pools, and fountains. The fossil remains are clothed with eyes, sinews, and muscles, and they again walk and talk. The past becomes the living present, and we find in imagination that there is no time or space. Through your imaginative faculty, you can be a companion of the most inspired writers of all time.

I gave a lecture on the 21st chapter of Revelation sometime ago in the Wilshire Ebell Theater in Los Angeles to our Sunday audience. The previous night while I was meditating on the inner meaning of the following verses, I intuitively and actually felt the presence and the intimate companionship of the mystic seer who wrote the inspired verses.

"And I John saw the holy city, new Jerusalem, coming down from God out of heaven, prepared as a bride adorned for her husband. And I heard a great voice out of heaven saying, Behold, the tabernacle of God is with men, and he will dwell with them, and be their God." (REV. 21:2, 2)

Can't you now walk down the corridor of your own mind, and there see, inwardly perceive, feel, and sense God's river of peace flowing through your mind? You are now in the Holy City—your own mind—inhabited by such lovely people as bliss, joy, faith, harmony, love, and goodwill. Your mind is clothed with God's radiant beauty; and your mood is exalted, noble, and Godlike. You are married mentally and spiritually to God and to all things good. You have on your wedding garment, because you are in tune with the Infinite, and God's Eternal Verities constantly impregnate your mind. In your imagination, you sense and feel that you are the tabernacle of God, and that His Holy Spirit saturates and fills every part of your being. Your imagination now becomes seized with a Divine frenzy. You become God-intoxicated, having received the Divine antibody, the Presence of God in the chamber of your heart.

You can look at a rock, and out of that rock through Divine Imagination you can reveal the Madonna, and portray a vision of beauty and a joy forever. Never permit your imagination to be used negatively; never distort or twist it. You can imagine sickness, accident, and loss and become a mental wreck. To imagine sickness and lack is to destroy your peace of mind, health, and happiness.

On board ship one time, I heard a passenger exclaim when looking at the setting sun, "I am so happy; I hope this lasts forever!"

How often have you seen a glorious sunrise, and perhaps you said, "I hope this lasts forever"? Nothing in this transitory world lasts eternally; however, the Truths of God last forever. Darkness follows night, but morning will come again. Twilight will also come. You do not want things to stand still. You do not want to stand still either, for there are new worlds within and without to conquer. Change eternal is at the root of all life.

You do not want to remain in a rut. Problems are life's way of asking you for an answer. The greatest joy and satisfaction is in overcoming, in conquering. Life would become unbearable and unendurable if we did not experience change. We would be bored by the monotony of things. You meet with night and day, cold and heat, ebb and flow, summer and winter, hope and despair, and success and failure. You find yourself moving through opposites; through your power to imagine what you wish to feel is to reconcile the opposites and bring peace to the mind.

In the midst of sorrow, grief, or the loss of a loved one, your imagination and faith—the two wings of the bird—take you aloft into the very Bosom of God, your Father, where you find peace, solace, and Divine rest for your soul.

In your imagination, you look into the very Face or Truth of God; and God wipes away all tears, and there shall be no more crying. All the mist and fog of the human mind dissolves in the sunshine of God's Love.

"And God shall wipe away all tears from their eyes; and there shall be no more death, neither sorrow, nor crying; neither, shall there be any more pain: for the former things are passed away. Behold I make all things new." (REV. 4:5.)

When the night is black, you see no way out; that is, when your problem is most acute, let your imagination be your savior.

"I will lift up mine eyes [imagination] unto the hills, from whence cometh my help." (PS. 121:1.) The hills are of an inner range—the Presence of God in you. When you seek guidance and inspiration, fix your eyes on the stars of God's Truth, such as "Infinite Intelligence leads and guides me," or "Divine Wisdom floods my mind, and I am inspired from on High."

There is a designer, an architect, and a weaver within you; it takes the fabric of your mind, your thoughts, feelings, and beliefs; and molds them into a pattern of life that brings you peace or discord, health or sickness. You can imagine a life that will take you up to the third heaven, where you will see unspeakable and unutterable things of God; or through the distorted, morbid use of your imagination, you can sink to the depths of degradation.

Man is the tabernacle of God, and no matter how low a man has sunk, the Healing Presence is there waiting to minister to him. It is within us waiting for us to call upon It. You can use your imagination in all business transactions in a wonderful way. Always imagine yourself in the other fellow's place; this tells you what to do. Imagine that the other is expressing all that you long to see him express. See him as he ought to be, not as he appears to be. Perhaps he is surly, sarcastic, bitter, or hostile; there may be many frustrated hopes and tragedies lurking in his mind. Imagine whatsoever things are lovely and of good report, and through your imagination you have covered him with the garment of God. God's world of ideals and God's infinite ideas are within him, waiting to be born and released. You can say if you wish, "God waits to be born in him." You can open the door, and kindle the fire of God's Love in that man's heart, and perhaps the spark you lit will burst into a Divine Fire.

The greatest and richest galleries of art in the world are the galleries of the mind devoted to God's Truths and Beauty. Leonardo Da Vinci, through his gift of imagination, meditated on Jesus and the Twelve Disciples, and what they meant. Lost in deep reverie, his imagination secreted the perfect pictures from the Infinite Reservoir within him, and due to his perfect focus, his inner eye glowed with an interior luminosity, so that he was inspired, and out of his Divine Imagery came the masterpiece *The Last Supper.*

You have visited a quiet lake or a mountaintop. Notice how the placid, cool, calm surface reflected the heavenly lights; so does the quiet mind of the spiritual man reflect God's interior Lights and Wisdom.

Picture your ideal in life; live with this ideal. Let the ideal captivate your imagination; let the ideal thrill you! You will move in the direction of the ideal that governs your mind. The ideals of life are like the dew of heaven that move over the arid areas of man's mind, refreshing and invigorating him.

The inspired writer's imagination was fired with Truth when he wrote: "There is a river the streams whereof shall make glad the city of God, the holy place of the tabernacles of the most High." (Ps. 46:4.)

By now you know that imagination is the river enabling *you* to flow back psychologically to God. The streams and rivulets are your ideas and feelings, plus the emanation of love and goodwill that goes forth from you to all men everywhere. Man looks out into the world; and he sees sickness, chaos, and man's inhumanity to man. The man with the disciplined imagination soars above all appearances, discord, and sense evidence, and sees the sublime principle of harmony operating through, in, and behind all things. He knows through his Divine imagery that there is an Everlasting Law of Righteousness behind all things, an Ever-Abiding Peace, a Boundless Love governing the entire Cosmos. These Truths surge through the heart, and are born of the eternal Truth that through the imagination pierces the outer veil, and rests in the Divine meaning of the way it is in God and Heaven.

Imagination was the workshop of God that inspired the writer of the following matchless, spiritual gems—which will go down through the corridor of time and live forever. For tender beauty and for Divine imagery, they are unsurpassed in dealing with the availability and Immanence of God's Presence:

"For he shall give his angels charge over thee, to keep thee in all thy ways." (Ps. 91:11.)

"Whither shall I go from thy spirit? or whither shall I flee from thy presence?"

"If I ascend up into heaven, thou art there. If I make my bed in hell, behold, thou art there."

"If I take the wings of the morning, and dwell in the uttermost parts of the sea; even there shall thy hand lead me, and thy right hand shall hold me."

Using the Subconscious Mind in Business

Long before our Bible was published, ancient wisdom said, "As a man imagines and feels, so does he become." This ancient teaching is lost in the night of time; it is lost in antiquity.

The Bible states: "As a man thinketh in his heart, so is he."

Legend relates that many thousands of years ago the Chinese wise men gathered together under the leadership of a great sage to discuss the fact that vast legions of brutal invaders were pillaging and plundering the land. The question to be resolved was: "How shall we preserve the ancient wisdom from the destruction of the invaders?"

There were many suggestions: Some thought that the ancient scrolls and symbols should be buried in the Himalayan mountains. Others suggested that the wisdom be deposited in monasteries in Tibet. Still others pointed out that the sacred temples of India were the ideal places for the preservation of the wisdom of their God.

The chief sage was silent during the entire discussion; in fact, he went to sleep in the midst of their talk and snored loudly, much to their dismay! He awakened in a little while, and said, "Tao [God] gave me the answer, and it is this: 'We will order the great pictorial artists of China—men gifted with Divine imagination [which is the workshop of God]—and tell them what we wish to accomplish. We will initiate them into the mysteries of Truth. They will portray or depict in picture form, the great Truths which shall be preserved for all time, and for countless generations yet unborn. When they are finished with the dramatization of the great Truths, Powers, Qualities, and Attributes of God through a series of picture cards, we will tell the world about a new game that has been originated. Men throughout the world for all time will use them as a game of chance, not knowing that through this simple device, they are preserving the sacred teaching for all generations.'" This was the origin of our own deck of cards.

The ancient Chinese sage, according to the legend, added, "If all the sacred writings were destroyed, they could again be resurrected at any time through the symbolic teachings and inner meanings of the various designs on the playing cards."

Imagination clothes all ideas and gives them form. Through the Divine artistry of imagination, these artists clothed all these ideas with pictorial form. In the act of imagination, that which is hidden in your deeper self is made manifest. Through imagination, what exists in latency or is asleep within you is given form in thought. We contemplate that which hitherto had been unrevealed.

Let us take some simple examples: When you were going to be married, you had vivid, realistic pictures in your mind. With your power of imagination, you saw the minister, rabbi, or priest. You heard him pronounce the words, you saw the flowers and the church, and you heard the music. You imagined the ring on your finger, and you traveled through your imagination on your honeymoon to Niagara Falls or Europe. All this was performed by your imagination.

Likewise, before graduation, you had a beautiful, scenic drama taking place in your mind; you had clothed all your ideas about graduation in form. You imagined the professor or the president of the college giving you your diploma. You saw all the students dressed in gowns. You heard your mother or father or your girl- or boyfriend congratulate you. You felt the embrace and the kiss; it was all real, dramatic, exciting, and wonderful. Images appeared freely in your mind as if from nowhere, but you know and must admit that there was and is an Internal Creator with Power to mold all these forms that you saw in your mind; and endow them with life, motion, and voice. These images said to you, "For you only we live!"

A young man said to me in the army before he was discharged, "I see my mother clearly. I can now imagine her welcome. I see the old home. Father is smoking a pipe. My sister is feeding the dogs. I can see every mark and corner of that home. I can even hear their voices."

Where do all these vivid pictures come from? Keats said that there is an ancestral wisdom in man, and we can, if we wish, drink of that old wine of heaven.

The spirit or God in you is the real basis of imagination. Once in an examination in London, I did not know the answer to an important question. I got still and quiet, and said over and over again slowly, meditating in a relaxed way, "God reveals the answer!" In the meantime, I went on answering the other questions, which were easy.

We know that when you relax the conscious mind, the subjective wisdom rises to the fore. In a short while, the picture of the answer came clearly into my mind. It was there in words like a page of a book, with the entire answer written out as a graph in the mind. A Mightier Wisdom than that of my conscious mind or intellect spoke through me.

I had a very religious school boy about 14 years old come to me. Whenever he had a problem, he said to me that he would imagine

Jesus was talking to him, giving him the answer to his problem, and telling him what to do. His mother was very ill; this boy was highly imaginative. He read the story of Jesus healing the woman with the fever. My little friend related to me, "Last night I imagined Jesus saying to me, 'Go thy way; thy mother is made whole!'" He made that drama of the mind so real, vivid, and intense that due to his faith and belief, he convinced himself of the truth of what he heard subjectively.

His mother was completely healed, yet she was considered at that time hopeless and beyond medical help.

Being a student of the laws of mind, you know what happened. He galvanized himself into the feeling of being one with his image, and according to his faith or conviction was it done unto him. There is only One Mind and One Healing Presence. As the boy changed his conviction about his mother and felt her perfect health, the idea of perfect health was resurrected in her mind simultaneously. He did not know anything about spiritual healing or the power of imagination. He operated the law unconsciously, and believed in his own mind that Jesus was actually talking to him; then, according to his belief, was it done unto him.

To believe something is to accept it as true. This is why Paracelsus said in the 16th century, "Whether the object of your belief be true or false, you will get the same results." There is only one spiritual, healing Principle and one Process of healing called *faith*. "According to your faith is it done unto you." There are many processes, methods, and techniques of healing, and all of them get results—not because of the particular technique or method, but because of imagination and faith in the particular process. They are all tapping the One Source of healing, which is God. The Infinite Healing Presence permeates all things and is omnipresent.

The voodoo doctor with his incantations gets results. So does the kahuna of Hawaii with his ministrations, the various branches

of New Thought and Christian Science, the Nancy School of
Medicine, osteopathy, and so on. All these schools of thought are
meeting levels of consciousness and are doing good.

Any method or process that alleviates human misery, pain,
and distress is good. Many churches practice the laying on of
hands; others make novenas and visit shrines; all are benefitted
according to their mental acceptance or belief.

When you are willing to stand alone with God and cease
completely giving power to external things; when you no longer
give power to the phenomenalistic world, which means to make
a world of effect a cause; and when all your allegiance is given to
the Spiritual Power within you, realizing it as the only Presence
and the only Cause, you will not need any props of any kind. The
Living Intelligence that made your body will respond immediately
to your faith and understanding; and you will have an instanta-
neous, spiritual healing. If you are not at that level of consciousness where you can grow a tooth through prayer, the obvious
thing to do is to go see a dentist. Pray for him and for a perfect,
Divine, oral adjustment. As long as you believe in external causes,
you will seek external remedies.

To illustrate further the power of imagination, I will tell you
about a close relative of mine who had tuberculosis. His lungs
were badly diseased, so his son decided to heal his father. He came
home to Perth, Western Australia, where his father lived, and said
to him that he had met a monk who sold him a piece of the true
cross, and that he gave him the equivalent of $500 for it. (This
young man had picked up a splinter of wood off the sidewalk, went
to a jeweler's, and had it set in a ring so that it looked real.) He told
his father that many were healed just by touching the ring or the
cross. He inflamed and fired his father's imagination to the point
that the old gentleman snatched the ring from him, placed it over
his chest, prayed silently, and went to sleep. In the morning, he was
healed; all the clinic's tests were negative.

You know, of course, that it was not the splinter of wood from the sidewalk that healed him. It was his imagination aroused to an intense degree, plus the confident expectancy of a perfect healing. Imagination was joined to faith or subjective feeling, and the union of the two brought about the healing. The father never learned the trick that had been played upon him; if he had, he probably would have had a relapse. He remained completely cured, and passed away 15 years later at the age of 89.

I know a businessman here in Los Angeles who has reached the top in his field. He told me that for 30 years, the most important decisions he ever made were based on his imaginary conversations with Paul. I asked him to elaborate, and he remarked that few people in the business world realized the wonderful guidance and counsel they could receive by dramatizing in their imagination that they were receiving counsel from the writers or great seers of the Bible.

I will quote this successful executive as accurately as I can: "Many times my decisions might have prospered the company or plunged it into bankruptcy. I vacillated, wavered, and got high blood pressure and heart disease. One day the idea came to me: Why not ask Jesus or Paul? I loved the Epistles of Paul, so when an important decision was to be made, I would imagine Paul was saying to me: 'Your decision is perfect; it will bless your organization. Bless you, my son! Keep on God's path.' After imagining I saw Paul and heard him, a wave of peace and inner tranquility would seize me; I was at peace about all decisions."

This was this businessman's way of receiving Divine Guidance by using his imagination to convince himself that right action was his. There is only one Principle of Intelligence in this world; all that is really necessary is to say and believe, "God is guiding me now, and there is only right action in my life."

The mind, as Troward tells you, works like a syllogism. If your premise is correct, the conclusion or result will correspond. The subjective reasons deductively only, and its sequence or conclusion is always in harmony with the premise. Establish the right premise in your mind; you will be subjectively compelled to right action. Inner movement of the mind is action. The external movements and action is the automatic response of the body to the internal motion of the mind. Hearing a friend or associate congratulate you on your wonderful decision will induce the movement of right action in your life.

The man who used St. Paul to impregnate his mind with the belief of right action was using the One Eternal Principle of Intelligence. His technique of arriving at that place in his mind does not really matter.

Goethe used his imagination wisely when confronted with difficulties and predicaments. His biographers point out that he was accustomed to filling many hours quietly holding imaginary conversations. It is well known that his custom was to imagine one of his friends before him in a chair answering in the right way. In other words, if he were concerned about any problems, he imagined that his friend was giving him the right or appropriate answer, accompanied with the usual gestures and tonal qualities of the voice, making the entire imaginary scene as real and vivid as possible.

I was very well acquainted with a stockbroker in New York City who used to attend my classes at Steinway Hall there. His method of solving financial difficulties was very simple. He would have mental, imaginary conversations with a multimillionaire banker friend of his who used to congratulate him on his wise and sound judgment, and compliment him on his purchase of the right stocks. He used to dramatize this imaginary conversation until he had psychologically fixed it as a form of belief in his mind.

Mr. Nicols, Ouspensky's student, used to say, "Watch your inner talking, and let it agree with your aim."

This broker's inner talking or speech certainly agreed with his aim to make sound investments for himself and his clients. He told me that his main purpose in his business life was to make money for others, and to see them prosper financially by his wise counsel. It is quite obvious that he was using the laws of mind constructively.

Prayer is a habit. This broker regularly and at frequent intervals during the day returned to the mental image in his mind; he made it a deep, subjective pattern. That which is embodied subjectively is objectively expressed. It is the *sustained* mental picture that is developed in the dark house of the mind. Run your mental movie often. Get into the habit of flashing it on the screen of your mind frequently. After a while it will become a definite, habitual pattern. The inner movie that you have seen with your mind's eye shall be made manifest openly: "He calleth things that be not as though they were, and the unseen becomes seen."

Many people solve their dilemmas and problems by the play of their imagination, knowing that whatever they imagine and feel as true, will and must come to pass.

Sometime ago, a certain young woman was involved in a complicated lawsuit that had persisted for five years. There was one postponement after another, with no solution in sight. At my suggestion, she began to dramatize as vividly as possible her lawyer having an animated discussion with her regarding the outcome. She would ask him questions, and he would answer her appropriately; then she condensed the whole thing down to a simple phrase, as suggested years ago by the French School of Mental Therapeutics. She had him repeat it over and over again to her. The phrase she said was: "There has been a perfect, harmonious solution. The whole case is settled outside court."

She kept looking at the mental picture whenever she had a spare moment. While in a restaurant for a cup of coffee, she ran the mental movie with gestures, voice, and sound equipment. She could imagine easily the sound of his voice, smile, and mannerisms. She ran the movie so often that it became a subjective pattern—a regular train track. It was written in her mind, or as the Bible says, it was "written in her heart and inscribed in her inward parts." Her conclusion was: "It is God in action," meaning all around harmony and peace. (*Harmony* is of God, and what you want in a legal case is a harmonious solution.)

In the science of imagination, you must first of all begin to discipline your imagination and not let it run riot. *Science* insists upon purity. If you wish a chemically pure product, you must remove all traces of other substances as well as extraneous material. You must, in other words, separate out and cast away all the dross.

In the science of imagination, you eliminate all the mental impurities, such as fear, worry, destructive inner talking, self-condemnation, and the mental union with other miscellaneous negatives. You must focus all your attention on your ideal, and refuse to be swerved from your purpose or aim in life. As you get mentally absorbed in the reality of your ideal, by loving and remaining faithful to it, you will see your desire take form in your world. In the book of Joshua it says, "Choose ye this day whom ye shall serve." Let your choice be, "I am going to imagine whatsoever things are lovely and of good report."

I know and have talked to many people who diabolically invert the use of their God-given faculty. The mother, for example, imagines that something bad has happened to her son, John, because he is late coming home. She imagines an accident, a hospital, Johnny in the operating room, and so on.

A businessman whose affairs are prospering, yet dwells on negativity, is another example of the destructive use of imagination. He comes home from the office, runs a motion picture in his mind of failure, sees the shelves empty, imagines himself going into bankruptcy, an empty bank balance, and the business closed down . . . yet all the time he is actually prospering. There is no truth whatsoever in that negative mental picture of his; it is a lie made out of whole cloth. In other words, the thing he fears does not exist save in his morbid imagination; the failure will never come to pass, except he keeps up that morbid picture charged with the emotion of fear. If he constantly indulges in this mental picture, he will, of course, bring failure to pass. He had the choice of failure or success, but he chose failure.

There are chronic worriers; they never seem to imagine anything good or lovely. They seem to know that something bad or destructive is always going to happen. They cannot tell you one reason why something good should and could happen; however, they are ready with all the reasons why something dire and evil should occur.

Why is this? The reason is simple: These people are habitually negative; that is, most of their thinking is of a negative, chaotic, destructive, morbid nature. As they continue to make a habit of these negative patterns of thought, they condition their subconscious mind negatively. Their imagination is governed by their dominant moods and feelings; this is why they imagine evil, even about their loved ones.

For example, if their son happens to be in the army, they imagine that he is going to catch cold, become an alcoholic, or become loose morally; or if he is in combat, they imagine he will be shot, and all manner of destructive images enter their minds. This is due to the hypnotic spell of habit, and their prayers are rendered null and void.

Make a choice now! Begin to think constructively and harmoniously. *To think* is to speak. Your thought is your word. Let your words be as a honeycomb, sweet to the ear, and pleasant to the bones. Let your words be "like apples of gold in pictures of silver." The future is the present grown up; it is your invisible word or thought made visible. Are your words sweet to the ear? What is your inner speech like at this moment? No one can hear you; it is your own silent thought. Perhaps you are saying to yourself, "I can't; it is impossible." "I'm too old now." "What chance have

I?" "Mary can, but I can't. I have no money. I can't afford this or that. I've tried; it's no use." You can see your words are not as a honeycomb; they are not sweet to your ear; they do not lift you up or inspire you.

Ouspensky was always stressing the importance of inner speech, inner conversation, or inner talking. It is really the way you feel inside, for the inside mirrors the outside. Is your inner speech pleasant to the bones? Does it exalt you, thrill you, and make you happy?

Bones are symbolic of support and symmetry. Let your inner talking sustain and strengthen you.

"But the word is very nigh unto thee, in thy mouth, and in thy heart, that thou mayest do it. See, I have set before thee this day life and good, and death and evil."

Decree now, and say it meaningly: "From this moment forward, I will admit to my mind for mental consumption only those ideas and thoughts that heal, bless, inspire, and strengthen me." Let your words from now on be as "apples of gold in pictures of silver." An apple is a delicious fruit. *Gold* means "power." *Pictures of silver* in the Bible means "your desires." The picture in your mind is the way you want things to be. It is the *picture* of your fulfilled desire. It could be a new position or health. Let your words, your inner silent thought, and feeling coincide and agree with the *picture of silver* or your desire. Desire and feeling joined together in a mental marriage will become the answered prayer.

Be sure you follow the imagination of the Bible, and let your words be sweet to the ear. What are you giving *your* ear to now? What are you listening to? What are you giving attention to? Whatever you give attention to will grow, magnify, and multiply in your experience.

"Faith cometh by hearing," Paul says. Listen to the great truths of God. Listen to the voice of God. What language does He speak in? It is not Gaelic, French, or Italian; but the universal language or mood of love, peace, joy, harmony, faith, confidence, and goodwill. Give your ear to these qualities and potencies of God. Mentally eat of these qualities; and as you continue to do so, you will be conditioned to those positive, enduring qualities, and the Law of Love will govern you.

You have heard this oft-repeated quotation: "Man is made in the image and likeness of God." This means that your mind is God's mind, as there is only One Mind. Your Spirit is God's Spirit, and you create in exactly the same way, and through the same law as God creates. Your individual world; that is, experiences, conditions, circumstances, environment, as well as your physical health, financial states, and social life, and so on, is made out of your own mental images and after your own likeness.

Like attracts like. Your world is a mirror reflecting back to you your inner world of thought, feeling, beliefs, and inner conversation. If you begin to imagine evil powers working against you, or that there is a jinx following you, or that other forces and people are working against you, there will be a response of your deeper mind to correspond with these negative pictures and fears in your mind; therefore, you will begin to say that everything is against you, or that the stars are opposed to you; or you will blame karma, your past lives, or some demon.

Truly the only sin is ignorance. Pain is not a punishment; it is the consequence of the misuse of your inner power. Come back to the one Truth, and realize that there is only One Spiritual Power, and It functions through the thoughts and images of your mind. The problems, vexations, and strife are due to the fact that man has actually wandered away after false Gods of fear and error. He must return to the center—the God-Presence within. Affirm now the sovereignty and authority of this Spiritual Power within you—the Principle of all life. Claim Divine guidance, strength, nourishment, and peace, and this Power will respond accordingly, I will now proceed to point out how you may definitely and positively convey an idea or mental image to your subconscious mind. The conscious mind of man is personal and selective. It chooses, selects, weighs, analyzes, dissects, and investigates. It is capable of inductive and deductive reasoning. The subjective or subconscious mind is subject to the conscious mind. It might be called a servant of the conscious mind. The subconscious obeys the order of the conscious mind. Your conscious thought has power. The power you are acquainted with is thought. In the back of your thought is Mind, Spirit, or God. Focused, directed thoughts reach the subjective levels; they must be of a certain degree of intensity. Intensity is acquired by concentration.

To *concentrate* is to come back to the center and contemplate the Infinite Power within you that lies stretched in smiling repose. To concentrate properly, you still the wheels of your mind and enter into a quiet, relaxed mental state. When you concentrate, you gather your thoughts together; and you focus all your attention on your ideal, aim, or objective. You are now at a focal or central point, where you are giving all your attention and devotion to your mental image. The procedure of focused attention is somewhat similar to that of a magnifying glass, and the focus it makes of the rays of the sun. You can see the difference in the effect of scattered vibrations of the sun's heat, and the vibrations that emanate from a central point. You can direct the rays of the magnifying glass so that it will burn up a particular object upon which it is directed. Focused, steadied attention of your mental images gains a similar intensity; and a deep, lasting impression is made on the sensitive plate of the subconscious mind.

You may have to repeat this drama of the mind many times before an impression is made, but the secret of impregnating the deeper mind is continuous or sustained imagination. When fear or worry comes to you during the day, you can always immediately gaze upon that lovely picture in your mind, realizing and knowing that you have operated a definite psychological law that is now working for you in the dark house of your mind. As you do so, you are truly watering the seed and fertilizing it, thereby accelerating its growth.

The conscious mind of man is the motor; the subconscious is the engine. You must start the motor, and the engine will do the work. The conscious mind is the dynamo that awakens the power of the subconscious.

The first step in conveying your clarified desire, idea, or image to the deeper mind is to relax, immobilize the attention, and get still and quiet. This quiet, relaxed, peaceful attitude of mind prevents extraneous matter and false ideas from interfering with your mental absorption of your ideal; furthermore, in the quiet, passive, receptive attitude of mind, effort is reduced to a minimum.

In the second step, you begin to imagine the reality of that which you desire. For example, you may wish to sell a home. In private consultation with real-estate brokers, I have told them of the way I sold my own home; they have applied it with remarkable results. I placed a sign in the garden in front of my home that read: "For sale by owner." The second day after placing the sign, I said to myself as I was going to sleep, "Supposing you sold the house, what would you do?"

I answered my own question, and I said, "I would take that sign down and throw it in the garage." In my imagination, I took hold of the sign, pulled it up from the ground, placed it on my shoulders, went to the garage, and threw it on the floor, saying jokingly to the sign, "I don't need you anymore!" I felt the inner satisfaction of it all, realizing that it was finished. The next day a man gave me a deposit of $1,000 and said, "Take your sign down; we will go into escrow now."

Immediately I pulled the sign up and took it into the garage. The outer action conformed to the inner. There is nothing new about this. "As within, so without," meaning according to the image impressed on the subconscious mind, so is it on the objective screen of your life.

This procedure or technique is older than our Bible. The outside mirrors the inside. External action follows internal action.

I was engaged by a very large organization to do some spiritual work for them. Through fraudulent means, others were trying to lay claim to their vast mining and other interests. They were harassing the company by legal trickery, and trying to get something for nothing. I told the lawyer to dramatize vividly in his imagination several times daily the president of the company that he represented congratulating him on the perfect, harmonious solution. As he sustained the mental picture through continuous mental application, the subjective wisdom gave him some new ideas—as he said, "Right out of the blue!" He followed these up, and the case was closed soon afterward.

If a person has a mortgage due at the bank and he does not have the money to cover it, and if he will faithfully apply this principle, the subconscious mind will provide him with the money. Never mind how, when, where, or through what source. The subjective mind has ways you know not of; its ways are past finding out. It is one of the instruments or tools that God gave man, so he could provide himself with all things necessary for his welfare. The man who hasn't the money to meet the mortgage can imagine himself depositing a check or currency required in the bank; that is, giving it to the cashier. The important point is to become intensely interested in the mental picture or imaginary act, making it real and natural. The more earnestly he engages his mind on the imaginary drama, the more effectually will the imaginary act be deposited in the bank of the subconscious mind. You can take a trip to the teller's window in your imagination, and make it so real and true that it will actually take place physically.

There is a young lady who comes to our Sunday-morning lectures regularly. She had to change buses three times; it took her one-and-a-half hours each Sunday to get there. In the sermon, I told how a young man prayed for a car and received one. She went home and experimented as follows: Here is her letter, in part, published with her permission:

"Dear Dr. Murphy:

This is how I received a cadillac [sic]; I wanted one to come to the lectures on Sunday and Tuesdays. In my imagination I went through the identical process I would go through if I were actually driving a car. I went to the show room, and the salesman took me for a ride in one. I also drove it several blocks. I claimed the Cadillac car as my own over and over again. I kept the mental picture of getting into the car, driving it, feeling the upholstery, etc., consistently for over two weeks. Last Sunday I drove to your meeting in a cadillac. My uncle in Inglewood passed away; left me his cadillac and his entire estate."

If you are thinking, *Well, I do not know of any way to get the money to pay off the mortgage*, don't worry about it. To worry means to strangle. Realize that there is a Power inherent within you that can provide you with everything you need when you call upon It. You can decree now with feeling and conviction: "My house is free from all debt, and wealth flows to me in avalanches of abundance." Do not question the manner in which the answer to your prayers will come. You will do the obvious things necessary, knowing that the subconscious intelligence is directing all your steps, for it knows everything necessary for the fulfillment of your dreams. You can also imagine a letter from them mortgage company informing you that you are paid up; rejoice in the image, and live with that imaginary letter in your mind until it becomes a conviction.

Become convinced now that there is a power within you that is capable of bringing what you imagine and feel as true into manifestation. Sitting idly by, daydreaming, and imagining the things you would like to possess, will not attract them to you. You must know and believe that you are operating a law of mind; become convinced of your God-given power to use your mind constructively to bring into manifestation the thing you desire.

Know what you want. The subconscious mind will carry out the idea, because you have a definite, clear-cut concept of what you wish to possess. Imagine clearly the fulfillment of your desire; then you are giving the subconscious something definite to act upon. The subconscious mind is the film upon which the picture is impressed. The subconscious develops the picture; and sends it back to you in a material, objectified form.

The camera is *you* consciously imagining the realization of your desire through focused attention. As you do so in a relaxed, happy mood, the picture is cast on the sensitive film of the subconscious mind. You also need a time exposure; it may be two or three minutes or longer depending on your temperament, feeling, and understanding. The important thing to remember is that it is not so much the time as the quality of your consciousness, degree of feeling, or faith. Generally speaking, the more focused and absorbed your attention is, and the longer the time, the more perfect will be the answer to your prayer. *Believe* that you have received, and ye shall receive. "Whatsoever ye shall ask in prayer, believing, ye shall receive." *To believe* is to accept something as true, or to live in the state of being it; as you sustain this mood, you shall experience the joy of the answered prayer!

3

How to Imagine Success

God is always successful in His undertakings. Man is equipped to succeed because God is within him. All the attributes, qualities, and potencies of God are within.

You were born to win, to conquer, and to overcome! The Intelligence, Wisdom, and Power of God are within you, waiting to be released, and enabling you to rise above all difficulties.

There are many men who quietly use the abstract term *success*, over and over many times a day until they reach a conviction that success *is* theirs. Remember that the *idea of success* contains all the essential elements of success. As a man repeats the word *success* to himself with faith and conviction, his subconscious mind will accept it as true of himself, and he will be under subjective compulsion to succeed.

We are compelled to express our subjective beliefs, impressions, and convictions. The ideal way to succeed is to know what you want to achieve. If you do not know your right place, or what you would like to do, you can ask for guidance on the question. The deeper mind will respond; as a result, you will find a push or tendency in a certain field of activity.

The deeper mind is responsive to your thought. The subconscious—sometimes called "subjective or deeper mind"—sets in operation its unconscious intelligence that attracts to the individual the conditions necessary for his success. Man should make it a special point to do the thing he loves to do. When you are happy in your endeavor, you are a success.

Accept the fact that you have an inner Creative Power. Let this be a positive conviction. This Infinite Power is responsive and reactive to your thought. To know, understand, and apply this principle causes doubt, fear, and worry to gradually disappear.

If a man dwells on the thought, for example, of failure, the thought of failure attracts failure. The subconscious takes the thought of failure as his request, and proceeds to make it manifest in his experience, because he indulges in the mental practice of conceiving failure. The subconscious mind is impersonal and nonselective.

A business friend of mine, a tailor by trade, has a favorite saying: "All I ever do is add. I never subtract." He means that *success* is a plus sign. *Add* to your growth, wealth, power, knowledge, faith, and wisdom.

Life is addition! Death is subtraction. You add to your life by imagining whatsoever things are true, lovely, noble, and Godlike. Imagine and feel yourself successful, and you must become successful. You are never a slave to circumstances, environment, or conditions. You are a master of conditions. You can become a victim of conditions by mentally acquiescing to things as they are. As you change your mind, you change conditions.

A movie actor told me once that he had very little education, but he had a dream as a boy of being a movie star. Out in the field mowing hay, or driving the cows home, or even when milking them, he said, "I would constantly imagine that I saw my name in big lights in a large theater. I kept this up for years until finally I ran away from home; got extra jobs in the motion picture field;

and the day came when I saw my name in great big lights, as I did when I was a boy!" Then he added, "I know the power of *sustained* imagination to bring success."

What does *success* imply to you? You want undoubtedly to be successful in your relationship with others. You wish to be outstanding in your chosen work or profession. You wish to possess a beautiful home, and all the money you need to live comfortably and happily. You want to be successful in your prayers, and in your contact with the Universal Power within you.

Imagine yourself doing the thing you long to do, and possessing the things you long to possess. Become imaginative; mentally participate in the reality of the successful state; enter into that state of consciousness frequently; make a habit of it; then you will find you will be guided to do everything necessary for the realization of your dream. Go to sleep feeling successful every night and perfectly satisfied. You will succeed eventually in implanting the idea of success in your subconscious mind.

I know a drugstore clerk who was a licensed pharmacist receiving $40 a week plus his commission on sales. "After 25 years," he told me, "I will get a pension and retire."

I said to him, "Why don't you own your own store? Get out of this place. Raise your sights! Have a dream for your children. Maybe your son wants to be a doctor or your daughter desires to be a musician."

His answer was that he had no money! He began to awaken to the fact that whatever he could conceive as true, he could give it conception.

The first step toward your goal is the *birth of the idea* in the mind, and the second step is the *manifestation of the idea.* He began to imagine that he was in his own store. He participated in the act mentally. He arranged the bottles, dispensed prescriptions, and imagined several clerks in the store waiting on customers. He visualized a big bank balance. Mentally he worked in that imaginary store. Like a good actor, he lived the role. (Act as though I am, and I will be.) This drugstore clerk put himself wholeheartedly into the act . . . living, moving, and acting in the assumption that his store was his.

The sequel was interesting. He was discharged from his position, went with a large chain store, became manager, and then district manager. He made enough money in four years to make a down payment on a drugstore of his own. He called it his "dream pharmacy." "It was," he said, "exactly the store he saw in his imagination." He became successful in his chosen field, and was happy doing what he loved to do.

The individual who habitually maintains a mental attitude of faith and expectancy of the best is bound to succeed and advance in life. The individual who is depressed, dejected, morbid, and despondent attracts failure all along the line. Fear is truly a lack of faith in Divine supply. It is faith misplaced. Fear is faith in the wrong thing. Fear is a belief in lack, or that man's good is being withheld from him.

"Son, thou are ever with me, and all that I hath is thine." All things you need are in the invisible. It could be said that all things needed are in the abstract. You must desire to be greater than you are, in order to advance in life. Desire comes first, followed by a recognition of the Power within you enabling you to manifest what you want. The subconscious mind is the medium through which all that you desire can be brought into objectivity. You are the one giving orders in the form of habitual thinking, feeling, opinions, and beliefs. The subconscious mind obeys the orders given by the conscious mind. If your conscious mind is opposed to all negative thoughts, they can make no impression upon your subconscious mind. You become immunized.

If, for example, you say, "I wish I were healthy, then I could be much more successful in my work;" begin *now* to realize that your body is your mind expressed. The subconscious mind is the builder of the body, and controls all its vital functions. Your conscious mind has the power to change any idea or group of thoughts held in the subconscious mind. You can impress the idea of health on your subconscious mind when you know that it can be done. A conviction and sincere belief is necessary. Affirmative statements establish a definite impression on the subconscious mind.

A wonderful way to impress the subconscious is through disciplined or scientific imagination. By illustration, if your knee is swollen and you are lame, imagine that you're doing the things you would do if you were in perfect health. You might say that I would go downtown on a bus, visit friends, ride horseback, go swimming, or hiking. First, in your imagination you go on these psychological journeys, making them as real and natural as possible. *Continue* to go on these psychological journeys! You know that self-motivation is yours. All movement is first of the mind or consciousness of man before any external movement can take place.

By example, the chair does not move of itself. You must impart motion to it. The same is true of your body. As you continue to do all the things you would do were you healed, this inner movement will cause the subconscious to build the body in accordance with the image back of it.

The following is a wonderful prayer for perfect health. A minister I knew in South Africa applied this prayer and healed himself. Several times a day he would affirm slowly and quietly, first making certain that he was completely relaxed mentally and physically: "The perfection of God is now being expressed through me. The idea of health is now filling my subconscious mind. The image that God has of me is a perfect image, and my subconscious mind re-creates my body in perfect accordance with the perfect image held in the mind of God." This is a simple, easy way of conveying the idea of perfect health to your subconscious mind.

You can develop confidence by knowing and realizing that nothing can prevent you from achieving success. Develop a certainty in your mind that this Inner Power can be called upon to overcome all obstacles. There must be an assurance and determination on your part that you can achieve and accomplish what you set out to do. This positive, affirmative attitude constitutes confidence.

You have heard the Biblical expression "According to your faith is it done unto you." Faith in God is the realization that there is only One Spiritual Power that is Omnipresent, Omniscient, Omnipotent, All Love, All Light, All Beauty, All Life, and An Ever-Present Help in time of trouble. Know that His Power responds to your thought.

Riches are Your Right

Contents

1

Consciousness of Health

How to Apply the Healing Principle

I will restore health unto thee, and I will heal thee of thy wounds, saith the Lord." The God in me has limitless possibilities. I know that all things are possible with God. I believe this and accept it whole-heartedly now. I know that the God-Power in me makes darkness light and crooked things straight. I am now lifted up in consciousness by contemplating that God indwells me.

I speak the word now for the healing of mind, body, and affairs; I know that this Principle within me responds to my faith and trust. "The Father doeth the works." I am now in touch with life, love, truth, and beauty within me. I now align myself with the Infinite Principle of Love and Life within me. I know that harmony, health, and peace are now being expressed in my body.

As I live, move, and act in the assumption of my perfect health, it becomes actual. I now imagine and feel the reality of my perfect body. I am filled with a sense of peace and well-being. Thank you, Father.

Prayer for Health

❧·❧

Jesus said, "Thy faith hath made thee whole."

I positively believe in the Healing Power of God within me. My conscious and subconscious mind are in perfect agreement. I accept the statement of truth which I positively affirm. The words I speak are words of spirit and they are truth.

I now decree that the Healing Power of God is transforming my whole body making me whole, pure, and perfect. I believe with a deep, inner certitude that my prayer of faith is being manifest now. I am guided by the Wisdom of God in all matters. The Love of God flows in transcendent beauty and loveliness into my mind and body, transforming, restoring, and energizing every atom of my being. I sense the peace that passeth understanding. God's Glory surrounds me, and I rest forever in the Everlasting Arms.

Wearing His Garment

❧·❧

I have found God in the sanctuary of my own soul. God is Life; that Life is my life. I know God is not a body; He is shapeless, timeless, and ageless; I see God in my mind's eye. Through understanding I see and look upon God in the same way that I see the answer to a mathematical problem.

I now rise to the awareness of peace, poise, and power. This feeling of joy, peace, and goodwill within me is actually the Spirit of God moving within me; It is God in action; It is Almighty. There is no power in external things to hurt me; the only Power resides in my own mind and consciousness.

My body is the garment of God. The Living Spirit Almighty is within me; It is absolutely pure, holy, and perfect. I know that this Holy Spirit is God, and that this Spirit is now flowing through me healing and making my body whole, pure, and perfect. I have complete power over my body and my world.

My thoughts of peace, power, and health have the Power of God to be realized within me now. "Blessed are the pure in heart: for they shall see God." I have seen and felt His Holy Presence; it is wonderful.

The Quiet Mind

God dwells at the center of my being. God is Peace; this Peace enfolds me in Its Arms now. There is a deep feeling of security, vitality, and strength underlying this peace. This inner sense of peace, in which I now dwell, is the Silent Brooding Presence of God. The Love and the Light of God watch over me, as a loving mother watches over the sleeping child. Deep in my heart is the Holy Presence that is my peace, my strength, and my source of supply.

All fear has vanished. I see God in all people; I see God manifest in all things. I am an instrument of the Divine Presence. I now release this inner peace; it flows through my entire being releasing and dissolving all problems; this is the peace that passeth understanding.

Mental Poise

Whither shall I go from thy Spirit? Or whither shall I flee from thy Presence? If I ascend up into heaven, thou art there: if I make my bed in hell, behold, thou art there. If I take the wings of the morning, and dwell in the uttermost parts of the sea: Even there shall thy hand lead me, and thy right hand shall hold me." I am now full of a Divine enthusiasm, because I am in the Presence of Divinity. I am in the Presence of All Power, Wisdom, Majesty, and Love.

The Light of God illumines my intellect; my mind is full of poise, balance, and equilibrium. There is a perfect mental adjustment to all things. I am at peace with my own thoughts. I rejoice in my work; it gives me joy and happiness. I draw continually upon my Divine Storehouse; for It is the only Presence and the only Power. My mind is God's mind; I am at peace.

The Peace of God

All is peace and harmony in my world, for God in me is "The Lord of Peace." I am the consciousness of God in action; I am always at peace. My mind is poised, serene, and calm. In this atmosphere of peace and goodwill which surrounds me, I feel a deep abiding strength and freedom from all fear. I now sense and feel the love and beauty of His Holy Presence. Day by day I am more aware of God's Love; all that is false falls away. I see God personified in all people. I know that as I allow this inner peace to flow through my being, all problems are solved. I dwell in God; therefore, I rest in the eternal arms of peace. My life is the life of God. My peace is the deep, unchanging peace of God; "It is the peace of God, which passeth all understanding."

The Gift of God

❧•❧

A merry heart maketh a cheerful countenance." The spirit of the Almighty pervades every atom of my being making me whole, joyous, and perfect. I know that all the functions of my body respond to this inner joy welling up within me. I am now stirring up the gift of God within me; I feel wonderful. The oil of joy and illumination anoint my intellect and become a lamp unto my feet.

I am now perfectly adjusted emotionally; there is a Divine equilibrium functioning in my mind, body, and affairs. I resolve from this moment forward to express peace and happiness to every person I meet. I know that my happiness and peace come from God; as I shed His light, love, and truth to others, I am also blessing and healing myself in countless ways. I radiate the sunshine of God's Love to all mankind. His Light shines through me and illuminates my path. I am resolved to express peace, joy, and happiness.

Controlling My Emotions

❧•❧

When a negative thought of fear, jealousy, or resentment enters my mind, I supplant it with the thought of God. My thoughts are God's thoughts, and God's Power is with my thoughts of good. I know I have complete dominion over my thoughts and emotions. I am a channel of the Divine. I now redirect all my feelings and emotions along harmonious, constructive lines. "The sons of God shouted for joy." I now rejoice to accept the ideas of God which are peace, harmony, and goodwill and I delight to express them; this heals all discord within me. Only God's ideas enter my mind, bringing me harmony, health, and peace.

God is Love. Perfect Love casteth out fear, resentment, and all negative states. I now fall in love with truth. I wish for all men everything I wish for myself; I radiate love, peace, and goodwill to all. I am at peace.

Overcoming Fear

❧❧

There is no fear, as "perfect Love casteth out fear." Today I permit Love to keep me in perfect harmony and peace with all levels of my world. My thoughts are loving, kind, and harmonious. I sense my oneness with God, for "In Him I live, move, and have my being."

I know that all my desires will be realized in perfect order. I trust the Divine Law within me to bring my ideals to pass. "The Father doeth the works." I am divine, spiritual, joyous, and absolutely fearless. I am now surrounded by the perfect peace of God; it is "The peace of God which passeth all understanding." I now place all my attention on the thing desired. I love this desire and I give it my whole-hearted attention.

My spirit is lifted into the mood of confidence and peace; this is the spirit of God moving in me. It gives me a sense of peace, security, and rest. Truly, "perfect Love casteth out fear."

The Holy Temple

Those that be planted in the house of the LORD shall flourish in the courts of our God." I am still and at peace. My heart and my mind are motivated by the spirit of goodness, truth, and beauty. My thought is now on the Presence of God within me; this stills my mind.

I know that the way of creation is Spirit moving upon Itself. My True Self now moves in and on Itself creating peace, harmony, and health in my body and affairs. I am Divine in my deeper self. I know I am a son of the living God; I create the way God creates by the self-contemplation of spirit. I know my body does not move of itself. It is acted upon by my thoughts and emotions.

I now say to my body, "Be still and quiet." It must obey. I understand this and I know it is a Divine Law. I take my attention away from the physical world; I feast in the House of God within me. I meditate and feast upon harmony, health, and peace; these come forth from the God-Essence within; I am at peace. My body is a temple of the Living God. "God is in His Holy Temple; let all the earth keep silent before Him."

2

Accept Abundance

God is the Eternal Now
(Using The Subconscious Mind)

I know that my good is this very moment. I believe in my heart that I can prophesy for myself harmony, health, peace, and joy. I enthrone the concept of peace, success, and prosperity in my mind now. I know and believe these thoughts (seeds) will grow and manifest themselves in my experience.

I am the gardener; as I sow, so shall I reap. I sow God-like thoughts (seeds); these wonderful seeds are peace, success, harmony, and goodwill. It is a wonderful harvest.

From this moment forward I am depositing in the Universal Bank (my subconscious mind) seeds or thoughts of peace, confidence, poise, and balance. I am drawing out the fruit of the wonderful seeds I am depositing. I believe and accept the fact that my desire is a seed deposited in the subconscious. I make it real by feeling the reality of it. I accept the reality of my desire in the same manner I accept the fact that the seed deposited in the ground will grow. I know it grows in the darkness; also, my desire or ideal grows in the darkness of my subconscious mind; in a little while, like the seed, it comes above the ground (becomes objectified) as a condition, circumstance, or event.

Infinite Intelligence governs and guides me in all ways. I meditate on whatsoever things are true, honest, just, lovely, and of good report. I think on these things, and God's Power is with my thoughts of Good. I am at peace.

The Way of Prayer

Thou shalt make thy way prosperous, and then thou shalt have good success." I now give a pattern of success and prosperity to the deeper mind within me, which is the law. I now identify myself with the Infinite Source of supply. I listen to the still, small voice of God within me. This inner voice leads, guides, and governs all my activities. I am one with the abundance of God. I know and believe that there are new and better ways of conducting my business; Infinite Intelligence reveals the new ways to me.

I am growing in wisdom and understanding. My business is God's business. I am Divinely prospered in all ways. Divine Wisdom within me reveals the ways and means by which all my affairs are adjusted in the right way immediately.

The words of faith and conviction which I now speak open up all the necessary doors or avenues for my success and prosperity. I know that "The Lord (Law) will perfect that which concerneth me." My feet are kept in the perfect path, because I am a son of the living God.

How to Realize the Abundant Life

※

I know that *to prosper* means to grow spiritually along all lines. God is prospering me now in mind, body, and affairs. God's ideas constantly unfold within me bringing to me health, wealth, and perfect Divine expression.

I thrill inwardly as I feel the Life of God vitalizing every atom of my being. I know that God's Life is animating, sustaining, and strengthening me now. I am now expressing a perfect, radiant body full of vitality, energy, and power.

My business or profession is a Divine activity, and since it is God's business, it is successful and prosperous. I imagine and feel an inner wholeness functioning through my body, mind, and affairs. I give thanks and rejoice in the abundant life.

The Prayer of Faith

※

The prayer of faith shall save the sick and God shall raise him up." I know that no matter what the negation of yesterday was, that my prayer or affirmation of truth will rise triumphantly over it today. I steadfastly behold the joy of the answered prayer. I walk all day long in the Light.

Today is God's day; it is a glorious day for me, as it is full of peace, harmony, and joy. My faith in the good is written in my heart and felt in my inward parts. I am absolutely convinced that there is a Presence and a perfect Law which receives the impress of my desire now and which irresistibly attracts into my experience all the good things my heart desires. I now place all my reliance, faith, and trust in the Power and Presence of God within me; I am at peace.

I know I am a guest of the Infinite, and that God is my Host. I hear the invitation of the Holy One saying, "Come unto me all ye that labor, and I will give you rest." I rest in God; all is well.

The Abundant Life

❖

Consider the Lilies of the field; they toil not, neither do they spin; yet Solomon in all of his glory was not arrayed as one of these." I know that God is prospering me in all ways. I am now leading the abundant life, because I believe in a God of abundance. I am supplied with everything that contributes to my beauty, well being, progress, and peace. I am daily experiencing the fruits of the spirit of God within me; I accept my good now; I walk in the light that all good is mine. I am peaceful, poised, serene, and calm. I am one with the source of life; all my needs are met at every moment of time and every point of space. I now bring "all the empty vessels" to the Father within. The fullness of God is made manifest in all the departments of my life. "All that the Father hath is mine." I rejoice that this is so.

Imagination, the Workshop of God

❖

Where there is no vision, the people perish." My vision is that I desire to know more of God and the way He works. My vision is for perfect health, harmony, and peace. My vision is the inner faith that Infinite Spirit leads and guides me now in all ways. I know and believe that the God-Power within me answers my prayer; this is a deep conviction within me.

I know that the mental picture to which I remain faithful will be developed in my subconscious mind and come forth on the screen of space.

I make it my daily practice to imagine only for myself and others that which is noble, wonderful, and God-like. I now imagine that I am doing the thing I long to do; I imagine that I now possess the things I long to possess; I imagine I am what I long to be. To make it real, I feel the reality of it; I know that it is so. Thank you, Father.

God's Will for Me

❧·❧

G od opens for me the windows of heaven, and pours me out a blessing."

God's will must be God-like; for that is the nature of God. God's will for me, therefore, is health, goodness, harmony, and abundance.

"If ye abide in me, and my words abide in you, ye shall ask what ye will, and it shall be done unto you." I am now enlightened by the truth; each day I am growing in wisdom and understanding. I am a perfect channel for the works of God; I am free from all worry and confusion. Infinite Intelligence within me is a lamp unto my feet. I know I am led to do the right thing; for it is God in action in all of my affairs.

The peace that passeth understanding fills my mind now. I believe and accept my ideal. I know it subsists in the Infinite. I give it form and expression by my complete mental acceptance. I feel the reality of the fulfilled desire. The peace of God fills my soul.

Abide in the Silence

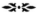

Jesus said, "God is a Spirit: and they that worship him must worship him in spirit and in truth."

I know and realize that God is a spirit moving within me. I know that God is a feeling or deep conviction of harmony, health, and peace within me; it is the movement of my own heart. The spirit or feeling of confidence and faith which now possesses me is the spirit of God and the action of God on the waters of my mind; this is God; it is the creative Power within me.

I live, move, and have my being in the faith and confidence that goodness, truth, and beauty shall follow me all of the days of my life; this faith in God and all things good is omnipotent; it removes all barriers.

I now close the door of the senses; I withdraw all attention from the world. I turn within to the One, the Beautiful, and the Good; here, I dwell with my Father beyond time and space; here, I live, move, and dwell in the shadow of the Almighty. I am free from all fear, from the verdict of the world, and the appearance of things. I now feel His Presence which is the feeling of the answered prayer, or the presence of my good.

I become that which I contemplate. I now feel that I am what I want to be; this feeling or awareness is the action of God in me; it is the creative Power. I give thanks for the joy of the answered prayer and I rest in the silence that "It is done."

To Be, to Do, and to Have

At the center of my being is Peace; this is the peace of God. In this stillness I feel strength, guidance, and the love of His Holy Presence. I am Divinely active; I am expressing the fullness of God along all lines. I am a channel for the Divine, and I now release the imprisoned splendor that is within. I am Divinely guided to my true expression in life; I am compensated in a wonderful way. I see God in everything and personified in all men everywhere. I know as I permit this river of peace to flow through my being, all my problems are solved. All things I need to fully express myself on this plane are irresistibly attracted to me by the Universal Law of attraction. The way is revealed to me; I am full of joy and harmony.

Love, Personality, Human and Family Relationships

God's Broadcast

※·※

"All ye are brethren, for one is your father." I always bring harmony, peace, and joy into every situation and into all of my personal relationships. I know, believe, and claim that the peace of God reigns supreme in the mind and heart of everyone in my home and business. No matter what the problem is, I always maintain peace, poise, patience, and wisdom. I fully and freely forgive everyone, regardless of what they may have said or done. I cast all my burdens on the God-self within; I go free; this is a marvelous feeling. I know that blessings come to me as I forgive.

I see the angel of God's Presence behind every problem or difficult situation. I know the solution is there and that everything is working out in Divine order. I trust the God-Presence implicitly; it has the *know-how* of accomplishment. The Absolute Order of Heaven and His Absolute Wisdom are acting through me now and at all times; I know that order is Heaven's first law.

My mind is now fixed joyously and expectantly on this perfect harmony. I know the result is the inevitable, perfect solution; my answer is God's answer; it is Divine; for it is the melody of God's broadcast.

Spiritual Rebirth

❦

Today I am reborn spiritually! I completely detach myself from the old way of thinking and I bring Divine love, light, and truth definitely into my experience. I consciously feel love for everyone I meet. Mentally I say to everyone I contact, "I see the God in you and I know you see the God in me." I recognize the qualities of God in everyone. I practice this morning, noon, and night; it is a living part of me.

I am reborn spiritually now, because all day long I practice the Presence of God. No matter what I am doing,—whether I am walking the street, shopping, or about my daily business,—whenever my thought wanders away from God or the good, I bring it back to the contemplation of His Holy Presence. I feel noble, dignified, and God-like. I walk in a high mood sensing my oneness with God. His peace fills my soul.

Love Frees

God is Love, and God is Life; this Life is one and indivisible. Life manifests Itself in and through all people; It is at the center of my own being.

I know that light dispels the darkness, so does the love of the good overcome all evil. My knowledge of the power of Love overcomes all negative conditions now. Love and hate cannot dwell together. I now turn the Light of God upon all fear or anxious thoughts in my mind, and they flee away. The dawn (light of truth) appears and the shadows (fear and doubt) flee away.

I know Divine Love watches over me, guides me, and makes clear the path for me. I am expanding into the Divine. I am now expressing God in all my thoughts, words, and actions; the nature of God is Love. I know that "perfect Love casteth out fear."

The Secret Place

He that dwelleth in the secret place of the most High shall abide under the shadow of the Almighty."

I dwell in the secret place of the most High; this is my own mind. All the thoughts entertained by me conform to harmony, peace, and goodwill. My mind is the dwelling place of happiness, joy, and a deep sense of security. All the thoughts that enter my mind contribute to my joy, peace, and general welfare. I live, move, and have my being in the atmosphere of good fellowship, love, and unity.

All the people that dwell in my mind are God's children. I am at peace in my mind with all the members of my household and all mankind. The same good I wish for myself, I wish for all men. I am living in the house of God now. I claim peace and happiness, for I know I dwell in the house of the Lord forever.

Overcoming Irritation

◆⋟·⋞◆

He that is slow to wrath, is of great understanding: but *he that* is hasty of spirit exalteth folly." I am always poised, serene, and calm. The peace of God floods my mind and my whole being. I practice the Golden Rule and sincerely wish peace and goodwill to all men.

I know that the love of all things which are good penetrates my mind casting out all fear. I am now living in the joyous expectancy of the best. My mind is free from all worry and doubt. My words of truth now dissolve every negative thought and emotion within me. I forgive everyone; I open the doorway of my heart to God's Presence. My whole being is flooded with the light and understanding from within.

The petty things of life no longer irritate me. When fear, worry, and doubt knock at my door, faith in goodness, truth, and beauty opens the door, and there is no one there. O, God, thou art my God, and there is none else.

Prayer of Gratitude

⋟⋞

O give thanks unto the Lord; call upon His name; make known His deeds among the people. Sing unto him, sing psalms unto him: talk ye of all his wondrous works. Glory ye in His holy name: let the heart of them rejoice that seek the Lord."

I give thanks sincerely and humbly for all the goodness, truth, and beauty which flow through me. I have a grateful, uplifted heart for all the good that has come to me in mind, body, and affairs. I radiate love and goodwill to all mankind. I lift them up in my thought and feeling. I always show my gratitude and give thanks for all my blessings. The grateful heart brings my mind and heart in intimate union with the creative Power of the Cosmos. My thankful and exalted state of mind leads me along the ways by which all good things come.

"Enter into his gates with thanksgiving, and into his courts with praise: Be thankful unto him, and bless his name."

How to Attract the Ideal Husband

⋟⋞

I know that I am one with God now. In Him I live, move, and have my being. God is Life; this life is the life of all men and women. We are all sons and daughters of the one Father.

I know and believe there is a man waiting to love and cherish me. I know I can contribute to his happiness and peace. He loves my ideals, and I love his ideals. He does not want to make me over; neither do I want to make him over. There is mutual love, freedom, and respect.

There is one mind; I know him now in this mind. I unite now with the qualities and attributes that I admire and want expressed by my husband. I am one with them in my mind. We know and love each other already in Divine Mind. I see the God in him; he sees the God in me. Having met him *within,* I must meet him in the *without;* for this is the law of my own mind.

These words go forth and accomplish whereunto they are sent. I know it is now done, finished, and accomplished in God. Thank you, Father.

How to Attract the Ideal Wife

God is one and indivisible. In Him we love, move, and have our being. I know and believe that God indwells every person; I am one with God and with all people. I now attract the right woman who is in complete accord with me. This is a spiritual union, because it is the spirit of God functioning through the personality of someone with whom I blend perfectly. I know I can give to this woman love, light, and truth. I know I can make this woman's life full, complete, and wonderful.

I now decree that she possesses the following qualities and attributes; i.e., she is spiritual, loyal, faithful, and true. She is harmonious, peaceful, and happy. We are irresistibly attracted to each other. Only that which belongs to love, truth, and wholeness can enter my experience. I accept my ideal companion now.

Divine Freedom

"If ye continue in my word, then are ye my disciples indeed: And ye shall know the truth, and the truth shall make you free." I know the truth, and the truth is that the realization of my desire would free me from all sense of bondage. I accept my freedom; I know it is already established in the Kingdom of God.

I know that all things in my world are projections of my inner attitudes. I am transforming my mind by dwelling on whatsoever things are true, lovely, noble, and God-like. I contemplate myself now as possessing all the good things of Life, such as peace, harmony, health, and happiness.

My contemplation rises to the point of acceptance; I accept the desires of my heart completely. God is the only Presence. I am expressing the fullness of God now. I am free! There is peace in my home, heart, and in all my affairs.

4

Expression

Prayer for World Peace

❖

eace begins with me. The peace of God fills my mind; the spirit of goodwill goes forth from me to all mankind. God is everywhere and fills the hearts of all men. In absolute truth all men are now spiritually perfect; they are expressing God's qualities and attributes. These qualities and attributes are Love, Light, Truth, and Beauty.

There are no separate nations. All men belong to the One Country—the One Nation which is God's Country. A country is a dwelling place; I dwell in the Secret Place of the Most High; I walk and talk with God—so do all men everywhere. There is only One Divine Family, and that is humanity.

There are no frontiers or barriers between nations, because God is One; God is indivisible. God cannot be divided against

Himself. The love of God permeates the hearts of all men everywhere. His Wisdom rules and guides the nation; He inspires our leaders and the leaders of all nations to do His will, and His will only. The peace of God which passeth all understanding fills my mind and the minds of all men throughout the cosmos. Thank you, Father, for Thy peace; it is done.

Predicting My Future

Thou madest him to have dominion over the works of thy hands." I know that my faith in God determines my future. My faith in God means my faith in all things good. I unite myself now with true ideas and I know the future will be in the image and likeness of my habitual thinking. "As a man thinketh in his heart so is he." From this moment forward my thoughts are on: "Whatsoever things are true, whatsoever things are honest, whatsoever things are just, whatsoever things are lovely, and of good report;" day and night I meditate on these things and I know these seeds (thoughts) which I habitually dwell upon will become a rich harvest for me. I am the captain of my own soul; I am the master of my fate; for my thought and feeling are my destiny.

My Destiny

I know that I mold, fashion, and create my own destiny. My faith in God is my destiny; this means an abiding faith in all things good. I live in the joy-out expectancy of the best; only the best comes to me. I know the harvest I will reap in the future, because all my thoughts are God's thoughts, and God is with my thoughts of good. My thoughts are the seeds of goodness, truth, and beauty. I now place my thoughts of love, peace, joy, success, and goodwill in the garden of my mind. This is God's garden and it will yield an abundant harvest. The glory and beauty of God will be expressed in my life. From this moment forward, I express life, love, and truth. I am radiantly happy and prosperous in all ways. Thank you, Father.

Impregnating the Subconscious Mind

The first step in the mental acceptance of your idea, desire, or image is to relax, immobilize the attention, get still, and quiet. This quiet, relaxed, peaceful attitude of mind prevents extraneous matter and false ideas from interfering with the mental absorption of your ideal; furthermore in the quiet, passive, receptive attitude of mind effort is reduced to a minimum. In this relaxed manner affirm slowly and quietly several times a day the following:

> *"The perfection of God is now being expressed through me. The idea of health is now filling my subconscious mind. The image God has of me is a perfect image, and my subconscious mind recreates my body in perfect accordance to the perfect image held in the mind of God."*

This is a simple, easy way of conveying the idea of perfect health to your subconscious mind.

The Balanced Mind

"Thou wilt keep him in perfect peace whose mind is stayed on thee, because he trusteth in thee." I know that the inner desires of my heart come from God within me. God wants me to be happy. The will of God for me is life, love, truth, and beauty. I mentally accept my good now and I become a perfect channel for the Divine.

I come into His Presence singing; I enter into His courts with praise; I am joyful and happy; I am still and poised.

The Still Small Voice whispers in my ear revealing to me my perfect answer. I am an expression of God. I am always in my true place doing the thing I love to do. I refuse to accept the opinions of man as truth. I now turn within and I sense and feel the rhythm of the Divine. I hear the melody of God whispering its message of love to me.

My mind is God's mind, and I am always reflecting Divine wisdom and Divine intelligence. My brain symbolizes my capacity to think wisely and spiritually. God's ideas unfold within my mind with perfect sequence. I am always poised, balanced, serene, and calm; for I know that God will always reveal to me the perfect solution to all my needs.

The Creative Word

"Be ye doers of the word, and not hearers only, deceiving your own selves." My creative word is my silent conviction that my prayer is answered. When I speak the word for healing, success, or prosperity, my word is spoken in the consciousness of Life and Power, knowing that it is done. My word has power, because it is one with Omnipotence. The words I speak are always constructive and creative. When I pray, my words are full of life, love, and feeling; this makes my affirmations, thoughts, and words creative. I know the greater my faith behind the word spoken, the more power it has. The words I use form a definite mold, which determine what form my thought is to take. Divine Intelligence operates through me now and reveals to me what I need to know. I have the answer now. I am at peace. God is Peace.

The Scientific Prayer

Before they call, I will answer; and while they are yet speaking, I will hear."

When I pray, I call on the Father, the Son, and the Holy Ghost; the Father is my own consciousness; the Son is my desire; the Holy Ghost is the feeling of being what I want to be.

I now take my attention away from the problem, whatever it may be. My mind and heart are open to the influx from on High.

I know the Kingdom of God is within me. I sense, feel, understand, and know that my own life, my awareness of being, my own I Amness, is the Living Spirit Almighty. I now turn in recognition to this One Who Forever Is; the Light of God illumines my pathway; I am Divinely inspired and governed in all ways.

Now I begin to pray scientifically in order to bring my desire into manifestation by claiming and feeling myself to be and to have what I long to be and to have. I walk in the inner silent knowing of the soul, because I know my prayer is already answered, as I feel the reality of it in my heart. Thank you, Father; it is done!

The Divine Answer

❖

I know that the answer to my problem lies in the God-Self within me. I now get quiet, still, and relaxed. I am at peace. I know God speaks in peace and not in confusion. I am now in tune with the Infinite; I know and believe implicitly that Infinite Intelligence is revealing to me the perfect answer. I think about the solution to my problems. I now live in the mood I would have were my problem solved. I truly live in this abiding faith and trust which is the mood of the solution; this is the spirit of God moving within me. This Spirit is Omnipotent; It is manifesting Itself; my whole being rejoices in the solution; I am glad. I live in this feeling and give thanks.

I know that God has the answer. With God all things are possible. God is the Living Spirit Almighty within me; He is the source of all wisdom and illumination.

The indicator of the Presence of God within me is a sense of peace and poise. I now cease all sense of strain and struggle; I trust the God-Power implicitly. I know that all the Wisdom and Power I need to live a glorious and successful life are within me. I relax my entire body; my faith is in His Wisdom; I go free. I claim and feel the peace of God flooding my mind, heart, and whole being. I know the quiet mind gets its problems solved. I now turn the request over to the God-Presence knowing It has an answer. I am at peace.

Prayer for Your Business

I now dwell on the Omnipresence and Omniaction of God. I know that this Infinite Wisdom guides the planets on their source. I know this same Divine Intelligence governs and directs all my affairs. I claim and believe Divine understanding is mine at all times. I know that all my activities are controlled by this indwelling Presence. All my motives are God-like and true. God's wisdom, truth, and beauty are being expressed by me at all times. The All-Knowing One within me knows what to do, and how to do it. My business or profession is completely controlled, governed, and directed by the love of God. Divine guidance is mine. I know God's answer, for my mind is at peace. I rest in the Everlasting Arms.

Right Action

I radiate goodwill to all mankind in thought, word, and deed. I know the peace and goodwill that I radiate to every man comes back to me a thousand fold. Whatever I need to know comes to me from the God-Self within me. Infinite Intelligence is operating through me revealing to me what I need to know. God in me knows only the answer. The perfect answer is made known to me now. Infinite Intelligence and Divine Wisdom make all decisions through me, and there is only right action and right expression taking place in my life. Every night I wrap myself in the Mantle of God's Love and fall asleep knowing Divine Guidance is mine. When the dawn comes, I am filled with peace. I go forth into the new day full of faith, confidence, and trust. Thank you, Father.

The Resurrection of My Desire

❧·❧

My desire for health, harmony, peace, abundance, and security is the voice of God speaking to me. I definitely choose to be happy and successful. I am guided in all ways. I open my mind and heart to the influx of the Holy Spirit; I am at peace. I draw successful and happy people into my experience. I recognize only the Presence and Power of God within me.

The Light of God shines through me and from me into everything about me. The emanation of God's Love flows from me; It is a healing radiance unto everyone who comes into my presence.

I now assume the feeling of being what I want to be. I know that the way to resurrect my desire is to remain faithful to my ideal, knowing that an Almighty Power is working in my behalf. I live in this mood of faith and confidence; I give thanks that it is done; for it is established in God, and all is well.

Achieving My Goal

❧·❧

In all thy ways acknowledge Him, and He will make plain thy path." My knowledge of God and the way He works is growing by leaps and bounds. I control and direct all my emotions along peaceful, constructive channels. Divine Love fills all my thoughts, words, and actions. My mind is at peace; I am at peace with all men. I am always relaxed and at ease. I know that I am here to express God fully in all ways. I believe implicitly in the guidance of the Holy Spirit within. This Infinite Intelligence within me now reveals to me the perfect plan of expression; I move toward it confidently and joyously. The goal and the objective that I have in my mind is good and very good. I have definitely planted in my mind the way of fulfillment. The Almighty Power now moves in my behalf; He is a Light on my path.

Business Problems

I know and believe my business is God's business; God is my partner in all my affairs; to me this means His light, love, truth, and inspiration fill my mind and heart in all ways. I solve all of my problems by placing my complete trust in the Divine Power within me. I know that this Presence sustains everything. I now rest in security and peace. This day I am surrounded by perfect understanding; there is a Divine solution to all my problems. I definitely understand everyone; I am understood. I know that all my business relationships are in accord with the Divine Law of Harmony. I know that God indwells all of my customers and clients. I work harmoniously with others to the end that happiness, prosperity, and peace reign supreme.

Principle in Business

My business is God's business. I am always about my Father's business which is to radiate Life, Love, and Truth to all mankind. I am expressing myself fully now; I am giving of my talents in a wonderful way. I am Divinely compensated.

God is prospering my business, profession, or activity in a wonderful way. I claim that all those in my organization are spiritual links in its growth, welfare, and prosperity; I know this, believe it, and rejoice that it is so. All those connected with me are Divinely prospered and illumined by the Light.

The Light that lighteth every man that cometh into the world leads and guides me in all ways. All my decisions are controlled by Divine Wisdom. Infinite Intelligence reveals better ways in which I can serve humanity. I rest in the Lord forever.

How to Solve Your Problems

—❖·❖—

What things soever you desire, when you pray, believe that ye receive them, and ye shall have them." I know that a problem has its solution within it in the form of a desire. The realization of my desire is good and very good. I know and believe that the Creative Power within me has the absolute Power to bring forth that which I deeply desire. The Principle which gave me the desire is the Principle which gives it birth. There is absolutely no argument in my mind about this.

I now ride the white horse which is the spirit of God moving upon the waters of my mind. I take my attention away from the problem and dwell upon the reality of the fulfilled desire. I am using the Law now. I assume the feeling that my prayer is answered. I make it real by feeling the reality of it. In Him I live, move, and have my being; I live in this feeling and give thanks.

Steps to Success

"Wist ye not that I be about my Father's business." I know that my business, profession, or activity is God's business. God's business is always basically successful. I am growing in wisdom and understanding every day. I know, believe, and accept the fact that God's law of abundance is always working for me, through me, and all around me.

My business or profession is full of right action and right expression. The ideas, money, merchandise, and contacts that I need are mine now and at all times. All these things are irresistibly attracted to me by the law of universal attraction. God is the life of my business; I am Divinely guided and inspired in all ways. Every day I am presented with wonderful opportunities to grow, expand, and progress. I am building up goodwill. I am a great success, because I do business with others, as I would have them do it with me.

The Triumph of Prayer

I now let go of everything; I enter into the realization of peace, harmony, and joy. God is all, over all, through all, and all in all. I lead the triumphant life, because I know that Divine Love guides, directs, sustains, and heals me. The Immaculate Presence of God is at the very center of my being; It is made manifest now in every atom of my body. There can be no delay, impediment, or obstructions to the realization of my heart's desire. The Almighty Power of God is now moving in my behalf. "None shall stay its hand, and say unto it, 'What doest thou?'" I know what I want; my desire is clear-cut and definite. I accept it completely in my mind. I remain faithful to the end. I have entered into the silent inner knowing that my prayer is answered and my mind is at peace.

About the Author

A native of Ireland who resettled in America, Joseph Murphy, Ph.D., D.D. (1898–1981) was a prolific and widely admired New Thought minister and writer, best known for his metaphysical classic, *The Power of Your Subconscious Mind*, an international bestseller since it first appeared on the self-help scene in 1963. A popular speaker, Murphy lectured on both American coasts and in Europe, Asia, and South Africa. His many books and pamphlets on the auto-suggestive and metaphysical faculties of the human mind have entered multiple editions—some of the most poignant of which appear in this volume. Murphy is considered one of the pioneering voices of affirmative-thinking philosophy.

www.ingramcontent.com/pod-product-compliance
Lightning Source LLC
Jackson TN
JSHW011941131224
75386JS00041B/1505